THIS JOURNAL BELONGS TO

....

MY BUCKET LIST

1. .... ☐
2. .... ☐
3. .... ☐
4. .... ☐
5. .... ☐
6. .... ☐
7. .... ☐
8. .... ☐
9. .... ☐
10. .... ☐
11. .... ☐
12. .... ☐
13. .... ☐
14. .... ☐
15. .... ☐
16. .... ☐
17. .... ☐
18. .... ☐
19. .... ☐
20. .... ☐

MY

BUCKET LIST

21 .... ☐
22 .... ☐
23 .... ☐
24 .... ☐
25 .... ☐
26 .... ☐
27 .... ☐
28 .... ☐
29 .... ☐
30 .... ☐
31 .... ☐
32 .... ☐
33 .... ☐
34 .... ☐
35 .... ☐
36 .... ☐
37 .... ☐
38 .... ☐
39 .... ☐
40 .... ☐

MY BUCKET LIST

41 .... ☐
42 .... ☐
43 .... ☐
44 .... ☐
45 .... ☐
46 .... ☐
47 .... ☐
48 .... ☐
49 .... ☐
50 .... ☐
51 .... ☐
52 .... ☐
53 .... ☐
54 .... ☐
55 .... ☐
56 .... ☐
57 .... ☐
58 .... ☐
59 .... ☐
60 .... ☐

MY BUCKET LIST

61 .... ☐
62 .... ☐
63 .... ☐
64 .... ☐
65 .... ☐
66 .... ☐
67 .... ☐
68 .... ☐
69 .... ☐
70 .... ☐
71 .... ☐
72 .... ☐
73 .... ☐
74 .... ☐
75 .... ☐
76 .... ☐
77 .... ☐
78 .... ☐
79 .... ☐
80 .... ☐

MY
BUCKET LIST

81 .... ☐
82 .... ☐
83 .... ☐
84 .... ☐
85 .... ☐
86 .... ☐
87 .... ☐
88 .... ☐
89 .... ☐
90 .... ☐
91 .... ☐
92 .... ☐
93 .... ☐
94 .... ☐
95 .... ☐
96 .... ☐
97 .... ☐
98 .... ☐
99 .... ☐
100 .... ☐

1

I Want To Do This Because

To Make This Happen I Need

Date Completed ....

Where ....

Solo - With ....

The Story

The Best Part

What I Learned From This

Would I Do It Again? ....

2

I Want To Do This Because

To Make This Happen I Need

Date Completed

Where

Solo - With

The Story

The Best Part

What I Learned From This

Would I Do It Again?

3

I Want To Do This Because

To Make This Happen I Need

Date Completed

Where

Solo - With

The Story

The Best Part

What I Learned From This

Would I Do It Again?

4

I Want To Do This Because

To Make This Happen I Need

Date Completed

Where

Solo - With

The Story

The Best Part

What I Learned From This

Would I Do It Again?

5

I Want To Do This Because

To Make This Happen I Need

Date Completed

Where

Solo - With

The Story

The Best Part

What I Learned From This

Would I Do It Again?

6

I Want To Do This Because

To Make This Happen I Need

Date Completed

Where

Solo - With

The Story

The Best Part

What I Learned From This

Would I Do It Again?

7

I Want To Do This Because

To Make This Happen I Need

Date Completed

Where

Solo - With

The Story

The Best Part

What I Learned From This

Would I Do It Again?

I Want To Do This Because

To Make This Happen I Need

Date Completed

Where

Solo - With

The Story

The Best Part

What I Learned From This

Would I Do It Again?

9

I Want To Do This Because

To Make This Happen I Need

Date Completed

Where

Solo - With

The Story

The Best Part

What I Learned From This

Would I Do It Again?

10

I Want To Do This Because

To Make This Happen I Need

Date Completed

Where

Solo - With

The Story

The Best Part

What I Learned From This

Would I Do It Again?

11

I Want To Do This Because

To Make This Happen I Need

Date Completed

Where

Solo - With

The Story

The Best Part

What I Learned From This

Would I Do It Again?

12

I Want To Do This Because

To Make This Happen I Need

Date Completed

Where

Solo - With

The Story

The Best Part

What I Learned From This

Would I Do It Again?

13

I Want To Do This Because

To Make This Happen I Need

Date Completed

Where

Solo - With

The Story

The Best Part

What I Learned From This

Would I Do It Again?

14

I Want To Do This Because

To Make This Happen I Need

Date Completed

Where

Solo · With

The Story

The Best Part

What I Learned From This

Would I Do It Again?

15

I Want To Do This Because

To Make This Happen I Need

Date Completed

Where

Solo - With

The Story

The Best Part

What I Learned From This

Would I Do It Again?

16

I Want To Do This Because

To Make This Happen I Need

Date Completed

Where

Solo - With

The Story

The Best Part

What I Learned From This

Would I Do It Again?

17

I Want To Do This Because

To Make This Happen I Need

Date Completed

Where

Solo - With

The Story

The Best Part

What I Learned From This

Would I Do It Again?

18

I Want To Do This Because

To Make This Happen I Need

Date Completed

Where

Solo - With

The Story

The Best Part

What I Learned From This

Would I Do It Again?

19

I Want To Do This Because

To Make This Happen I Need

Date Completed

Where

Solo - With

The Story

The Best Part

What I Learned From This

Would I Do It Again?

20

I Want To Do This Because

To Make This Happen I Need

Date Completed

Where

Solo · With

The Story

The Best Part

What I Learned From This

Would I Do It Again?

21

I Want To Do This Because

To Make This Happen I Need

Date Completed

Where

Solo • With

The Story

The Best Part

What I Learned From This

Would I Do It Again?

22

I Want To Do This Because

To Make This Happen I Need

Date Completed

Where

Solo - With

The Story

The Best Part

What I Learned From This

Would I Do It Again?

23

I Want To Do This Because

To Make This Happen I Need

Date Completed

Where

Solo · With

The Story

The Best Part

What I Learned From This

Would I Do It Again?

24

I Want To Do This Because

To Make This Happen I Need

Date Completed

Where

Solo · With

The Story

The Best Part

What I Learned From This

Would I Do It Again?

25

I Want To Do This Because

To Make This Happen I Need

Date Completed

Where

Solo - With

The Story

The Best Part

What I Learned From This

Would I Do It Again?

26

I Want To Do This Because

To Make This Happen I Need

Date Completed

Where

Solo - With

The Story

The Best Part

What I Learned From This

Would I Do It Again?

27

I Want To Do This Because

To Make This Happen I Need

Date Completed

Where

Solo - With

The Story

The Best Part

What I Learned From This

Would I Do It Again?

28

I Want To Do This Because

To Make This Happen I Need

Date Completed

Where

Solo - With

The Story

The Best Part

What I Learned From This

Would I Do It Again?

29

I Want To Do This Because

To Make This Happen I Need

Date Completed

Where

Solo - With

The Story

The Best Part

What I Learned From This

Would I Do It Again?

30

I Want To Do This Because

To Make This Happen I Need

Date Completed

Where

Solo · With

The Story

The Best Part

What I Learned From This

Would I Do It Again?

31

I Want To Do This Because

To Make This Happen I Need

Date Completed

Where

Solo - With

The Story

The Best Part

What I Learned From This

Would I Do It Again?

32

I Want To Do This Because

To Make This Happen I Need

Date Completed

Where

Solo - With

The Story

The Best Part

What I Learned From This

Would I Do It Again?

33

I Want To Do This Because

To Make This Happen I Need

Date Completed

Where

Solo - With

The Story

The Best Part

What I Learned From This

Would I Do It Again?

34

I Want To Do This Because

To Make This Happen I Need

Date Completed

Where

Solo - With

The Story

The Best Part

What I Learned From This

Would I Do It Again?

35

I Want To Do This Because

To Make This Happen I Need

Date Completed

Where

Solo - With

The Story

The Best Part

What I Learned From This

Would I Do It Again?

36

I Want To Do This Because

To Make This Happen I Need

Date Completed

Where

Solo - With

The Story

The Best Part

What I Learned From This

Would I Do It Again?

37

I Want To Do This Because

To Make This Happen I Need

Date Completed

Where

Solo - With

The Story

The Best Part

What I Learned From This

Would I Do It Again?

38

I Want To Do This Because

To Make This Happen I Need

Date Completed

Where

Solo - With

The Story

The Best Part

What I Learned From This

Would I Do It Again?

39

I Want To Do This Because

To Make This Happen I Need

Date Completed

Where

Solo - With

The Story

The Best Part

What I Learned From This

Would I Do It Again?

40

....

I Want To Do This Because

....

To Make This Happen I Need

....

Date Completed ....

Where ....

Solo - With ....

The Story

....

....

The Best Part

....

....

What I Learned From This

....

....

Would I Do It Again? ....

41

I Want To Do This Because

To Make This Happen I Need

Date Completed

Where

Solo - With

The Story

The Best Part

What I Learned From This

Would I Do It Again?

42

....

I Want To Do This Because

....

To Make This Happen I Need

....

Date Completed ....

Where ....

Solo - With ....

The Story

....

....

The Best Part

....

....

What I Learned From This

....

....

Would I Do It Again? ....

43

I Want To Do This Because

To Make This Happen I Need

Date Completed

Where

Solo - With

The Story

The Best Part

What I Learned From This

Would I Do It Again?

44

I Want To Do This Because

To Make This Happen I Need

Date Completed

Where

Solo - With

The Story

The Best Part

What I Learned From This

Would I Do It Again?

45

I Want To Do This Because

To Make This Happen I Need

Date Completed

Where

Solo - With

The Story

The Best Part

What I Learned From This

Would I Do It Again?

46

I Want To Do This Because

To Make This Happen I Need

Date Completed

Where

Solo - With

The Story

The Best Part

What I Learned From This

Would I Do It Again?

47

I Want To Do This Because

To Make This Happen I Need

Date Completed

Where

Solo - With

The Story

The Best Part

What I Learned From This

Would I Do It Again?

48

I Want To Do This Because

To Make This Happen I Need

Date Completed

Where

Solo · With

The Story

The Best Part

What I Learned From This

Would I Do It Again?

49

I Want To Do This Because

To Make This Happen I Need

Date Completed

Where

Solo - With

The Story

The Best Part

What I Learned From This

Would I Do It Again?

50

I Want To Do This Because

To Make This Happen I Need

Date Completed

Where

Solo - With

The Story

The Best Part

What I Learned From This

Would I Do It Again?

51

....

I Want To Do This Because

....

To Make This Happen I Need

....

Date Completed ....

Where ....

Solo - With ....

The Story

....

....

The Best Part

....

....

What I Learned From This

....

....

Would I Do It Again? ....

52

I Want To Do This Because

To Make This Happen I Need

Date Completed

Where

Solo - With

The Story

The Best Part

What I Learned From This

Would I Do It Again?

53

I Want To Do This Because

To Make This Happen I Need

Date Completed

Where

Solo - With

The Story

The Best Part

What I Learned From This

Would I Do It Again?

54

I Want To Do This Because

To Make This Happen I Need

Date Completed

Where

Solo - With

The Story

The Best Part

What I Learned From This

Would I Do It Again?

55

I Want To Do This Because

To Make This Happen I Need

Date Completed

Where

Solo - With

The Story

The Best Part

What I Learned From This

Would I Do It Again?

56

I Want To Do This Because

To Make This Happen I Need

Date Completed

Where

Solo - With

The Story

The Best Part

What I Learned From This

Would I Do It Again?

57

I Want To Do This Because

To Make This Happen I Need

Date Completed

Where

Solo - With

The Story

The Best Part

What I Learned From This

Would I Do It Again?

58

I Want To Do This Because

To Make This Happen I Need

Date Completed

Where

Solo - With

The Story

The Best Part

What I Learned From This

Would I Do It Again?

59

I Want To Do This Because

To Make This Happen I Need

Date Completed

Where

Solo - With

The Story

The Best Part

What I Learned From This

Would I Do It Again?

60

I Want To Do This Because

To Make This Happen I Need

Date Completed

Where

Solo · With

The Story

The Best Part

What I Learned From This

Would I Do It Again?

61

I Want To Do This Because

To Make This Happen I Need

Date Completed

Where

Solo - With

The Story

The Best Part

What I Learned From This

Would I Do It Again?

62

I Want To Do This Because

To Make This Happen I Need

Date Completed

Where

Solo - With

The Story

The Best Part

What I Learned From This

Would I Do It Again?

63

I Want To Do This Because

To Make This Happen I Need

Date Completed

Where

Solo - With

The Story

The Best Part

What I Learned From This

Would I Do It Again?

64

I Want To Do This Because

To Make This Happen I Need

Date Completed

Where

Solo - With

The Story

The Best Part

What I Learned From This

Would I Do It Again?

65

I Want To Do This Because

To Make This Happen I Need

Date Completed

Where

Solo - With

The Story

The Best Part

What I Learned From This

Would I Do It Again?

66

I Want To Do This Because

To Make This Happen I Need

Date Completed

Where

Solo - With

The Story

The Best Part

What I Learned From This

Would I Do It Again?

67

....

I Want To Do This Because

....

To Make This Happen I Need

....

Date Completed ....

Where ....

Solo - With ....

The Story

....

....

The Best Part

....

....

What I Learned From This

....

....

Would I Do It Again? ....

68

I Want To Do This Because

To Make This Happen I Need

Date Completed

Where

Solo - With

The Story

The Best Part

What I Learned From This

Would I Do It Again?

69

I Want To Do This Because

To Make This Happen I Need

Date Completed

Where

Solo - With

The Story

The Best Part

What I Learned From This

Would I Do It Again?

70

I Want To Do This Because

To Make This Happen I Need

Date Completed

Where

Solo - With

The Story

The Best Part

What I Learned From This

Would I Do It Again?

71

I Want To Do This Because

To Make This Happen I Need

Date Completed

Where

Solo - With

The Story

The Best Part

What I Learned From This

Would I Do It Again?

72

I Want To Do This Because

To Make This Happen I Need

Date Completed

Where

Solo - With

The Story

The Best Part

What I Learned From This

Would I Do It Again?

73

I Want To Do This Because

To Make This Happen I Need

Date Completed

Where

Solo - With

The Story

The Best Part

What I Learned From This

Would I Do It Again?

74

I Want To Do This Because

To Make This Happen I Need

Date Completed

Where

Solo - With

The Story

The Best Part

What I Learned From This

Would I Do It Again?

75

I Want To Do This Because

To Make This Happen I Need

Date Completed

Where

Solo - With

The Story

The Best Part

What I Learned From This

Would I Do It Again?

76

I Want To Do This Because

To Make This Happen I Need

Date Completed

Where

Solo - With

The Story

The Best Part

What I Learned From This

Would I Do It Again?

77

I Want To Do This Because

To Make This Happen I Need

Date Completed

Where

Solo - With

The Story

The Best Part

What I Learned From This

Would I Do It Again?

78

I Want To Do This Because

To Make This Happen I Need

Date Completed

Where

Solo - With

The Story

The Best Part

What I Learned From This

Would I Do It Again?

79

I Want To Do This Because

To Make This Happen I Need

Date Completed

Where

Solo - With

The Story

The Best Part

What I Learned From This

Would I Do It Again?

80

I Want To Do This Because

To Make This Happen I Need

Date Completed

Where

Solo - With

The Story

The Best Part

What I Learned From This

Would I Do It Again?

81

I Want To Do This Because

To Make This Happen I Need

Date Completed

Where

Solo - With

The Story

The Best Part

What I Learned From This

Would I Do It Again?

82

I Want To Do This Because

To Make This Happen I Need

Date Completed

Where

Solo - With

The Story

The Best Part

What I Learned From This

Would I Do It Again?

83

I Want To Do This Because

To Make This Happen I Need

Date Completed

Where

Solo - With

The Story

The Best Part

What I Learned From This

Would I Do It Again?

84

....

I Want To Do This Because

....

To Make This Happen I Need

....

Date Completed ....

Where ....

Solo - With ....

The Story

....

....

The Best Part

....

....

What I Learned From This

....

....

Would I Do It Again? ....

85

I Want To Do This Because

To Make This Happen I Need

Date Completed

Where

Solo - With

The Story

The Best Part

What I Learned From This

Would I Do It Again?

86

....

I Want To Do This Because

....

To Make This Happen I Need

....

Date Completed ....

Where ....

Solo - With ....

The Story

....

....

The Best Part

....

....

What I Learned From This

....

....

Would I Do It Again? ....

87

I WANT TO DO THIS BECAUSE

TO MAKE THIS HAPPEN I NEED

DATE COMPLETED

WHERE

SOLO - WITH

THE STORY

THE BEST PART

WHAT I LEARNED FROM THIS

WOULD I DO IT AGAIN?

I Want To Do This Because

To Make This Happen I Need

Date Completed

Where

Solo - With

The Story

The Best Part

What I Learned From This

Would I Do It Again?

89

I Want To Do This Because

To Make This Happen I Need

Date Completed

Where

Solo - With

The Story

The Best Part

What I Learned From This

Would I Do It Again?

90

I Want To Do This Because

To Make This Happen I Need

Date Completed

Where

Solo - With

The Story

The Best Part

What I Learned From This

Would I Do It Again?

91

I Want To Do This Because

To Make This Happen I Need

Date Completed

Where

Solo · With

The Story

The Best Part

What I Learned From This

Would I Do It Again?

92

I Want To Do This Because

To Make This Happen I Need

Date Completed

Where

Solo - With

The Story

The Best Part

What I Learned From This

Would I Do It Again?

93

I Want To Do This Because

To Make This Happen I Need

Date Completed

Where

Solo - With

The Story

The Best Part

What I Learned From This

Would I Do It Again?

94

....

I Want To Do This Because

....

To Make This Happen I Need

....

Date Completed ....

Where ....

Solo - With ....

The Story

....

....

The Best Part

....

....

What I Learned From This

....

....

Would I Do It Again? ....

95

I Want To Do This Because

To Make This Happen I Need

Date Completed

Where

Solo - With

The Story

The Best Part

What I Learned From This

Would I Do It Again?

96

I Want To Do This Because

To Make This Happen I Need

Date Completed

Where

Solo - With

The Story

The Best Part

What I Learned From This

Would I Do It Again?

97

....

I Want To Do This Because

....

To Make This Happen I Need

....

Date Completed ....

Where ....

Solo - With ....

The Story

....

....

The Best Part

....

....

What I Learned From This

....

....

Would I Do It Again? ....

98

I Want To Do This Because

To Make This Happen I Need

Date Completed

Where

Solo - With

The Story

The Best Part

What I Learned From This

Would I Do It Again?

99

I Want To Do This Because

To Make This Happen I Need

Date Completed

Where

Solo - With

The Story

The Best Part

What I Learned From This

Would I Do It Again?

100

I Want To Do This Because

To Make This Happen I Need

Date Completed

Where

Solo - With

The Story

The Best Part

What I Learned From This

Would I Do It Again?